W9-AFN-434

MEASURES *of* SUCCESS®

A Comprehensive Musicianship Band Method

DEBORAH A. SHELDON • BRIAN BALMAGES • TIMOTHY LOEST • ROBERT SHELDON

PERCUSSION WRITTEN AND EDITED BY DAVID COLLIER

Welcome to *Measures of Success* and the amazing world of instrumental music!
You are about to begin an exciting musical journey full of rewards and challenges.
As you practice, you will find yourself sharing the gift of music with family, friends,
and audiences. So get ready—your path to success begins now!

HISTORY OF THE TROMBONE

The trombone first appeared in the mid 1400s and was probably developed from the long straight
trumpets that predated it. The early trombone was called a sackbut; the word sackbut comes from two
French words meaning to pull and to push (think of a trombone slide!). The trombone's low sound
was so effective in balancing out harmonies that it became a regular part of the orchestra in the 1700s.
Its ability to project also made it suitable for use in military bands. The modern trombone, with its
beautifully rich tone, is found in many ensembles, including jazz and rock bands. The two most common
types of trombones are the tenor trombone and the bass trombone. Trombones are members of the
brass family because they are made from brass and use a funnel-shaped mouthpiece. Sound is created
when players buzz their lips inside the mouthpiece. Sound is changed when players move the main
slide in and out, which is different from other brass instruments that are fitted with valves. The trombone
is the only instrument that can slide between notes making a very familiar sound called a *glissando*.

Production: Frank J. Hackinson
Production Coordinators: Ken Mattis, Brian Balmages, and Philip Groeber
Cover Design and Interior Line Drawings: Danielle Taylor and Adrianne Hirosky
Interior Layout and Design: Andi Whitmer
Engraving: Tempo Music Press, Inc.
Printer: Tempo Music Press, Inc.

ISBN-13: 978-1-56939-814-2

THE FJH MUSIC COMPANY INC.
Frank J. Hackinson

TROMBONE ASSEMBLY

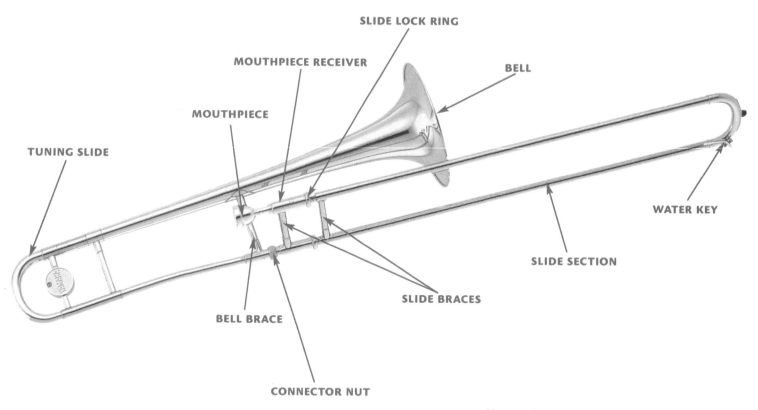

SLIDE LOCK RING

MOUTHPIECE RECEIVER

BELL

MOUTHPIECE

TUNING SLIDE

WATER KEY

SLIDE SECTION

SLIDE BRACES

BELL BRACE

CONNECTOR NUT

Photograph courtesy of Yamaha Corporation of America

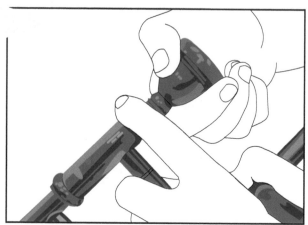

STEP 1

Lay your case flat on the floor. Open your case right side up.

STEP 2

Lock the slide using the slide lock ring. Pick up the slide with your right hand and the bell section with your left hand. Fasten both parts together so that the slide is at a 90° angle to the bell section. Tighten the connector nut to hold these parts together.

STEP 3

Pick up the mouthpiece with your right hand and insert the mouthpiece shank into the mouthpiece receiver. Give the mouthpiece a gentle twist so that the shank grips inside the receiver pipe.

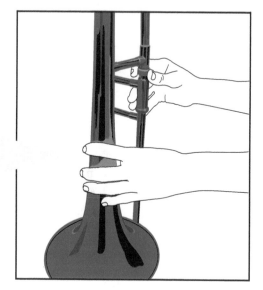

CHECK IT OUT!

POSTURE CHECKLIST

- Sit on the front edge of the chair
- Feet flat on the floor
- Sit straight and tall
- Shoulders relaxed
- Elbows comfortably away from your sides

HAND POSITION CHECKLIST

- Left thumb grips the underside of the bell brace while the left index finger sits on the mouthpiece receiver (remaining fingers wrap around the first slide brace)
- Second slide brace is secured between the right thumb and first two fingers
- Left hand supports the trombone, while relaxed right wrist and hand moves the slide

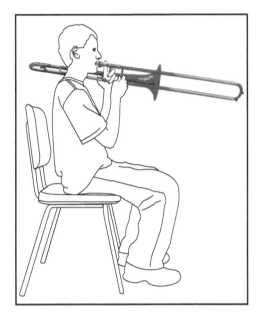

EMBOUCHURE CHECKLIST

- Lips are positioned as if saying "M"
- Keep the chin flat, corners firm, and center relaxed
- Blow a focused stream of air through the center of the lips to create a buzz
- Keep the space between the top and bottom teeth open (do not clench)

TROMBONE SUPPLIES

- slide oil
- tuning slide grease
- mouthpiece brush
- soft cloth
- cleaning snake

TROMBONE CARE

DAILY

- Blow excess moisture out of the trombone before putting it away
- Wipe away fingerprints with a soft cloth
- Oil slide (use sparingly only when needed)

WEEKLY

- Clean mouthpiece with mouthpiece brush, warm water, and a dab of liquid soap

MONTHLY

- Wipe tuning slide clean, then lubricate with slide grease (use sparingly)

YEARLY

- Take your trombone to an authorized repair shop for a chemical bath and tune-up

NEVER

- Never apply cleaners or polishes to your trombone
- Never try to remove a stuck or frozen mouthpiece or tuning slide - leave this for your teacher or the repair shop
- Never smack the mouthpiece while it is on the mouthpiece receiver pipe
- Never over-lubricate the slide
- Never leave your trombone unattended, or on the floor or a chair
- Never keep anything in your case except for your instrument and care supplies

PRELUDE: SOUNDS BEFORE SYMBOLS

BREATHING

The key to playing a wind instrument well begins with taking a good breath. With just your mouthpiece, take a full, relaxed breath and play a steady tone. How long can you hold it?

THEORY

PITCH, BEAT, AND RHYTHM

Pitch is the highness or lowness of a note or tone. The **beat** is the pulse of the music.
Rhythm is a pattern of short or long sounds (or silences) that fit with a steady beat.

ARTICULATION

Articulation is how the tongue and the air begin a note. Your director will show you how to articulate a note.

With just your mouthpiece, play some of the familiar songs below. Articulate clearly!

Bingo	**Jingle Bells**	**London Bridge**
Mary Had a Little Lamb	**Old MacDonald**	**Twinkle, Twinkle Little Star**

MAKING MUSIC

With your director's help, assemble your trombone carefully. You are now ready for your first three notes!

 NEW NOTE! **D** **4** (4th position)   **NEW NOTE!** **C** **6** (6th position)   **NEW NOTE!** **Bb** **1** (1st position)

Hold each note with a good sound until you are comfortable with it. Next, articulate each note four times and then rest for four beats. Remember to focus on posture, hand position, and tone quality.

AND WE'RE OFF!
(hold) (rest)
D ——→ | – – – – | D D D D | – – – – | (repeat this with your other two new notes)
1 2 3 4 1 2 3 4 1 2 3 4 1 2 3 4

AU CLAIRE DE LA LUNE
Bb Bb Bb C | D – C – | Bb D C C | Bb —→ – – |
1 2 3 4 1 2 3 4 1 2 3 4 1 2 3 4

HOT CROSS BUNS
D —→ C —→ | Bb —→ – – | D —→ C —→ | Bb —→ – – | Bb Bb Bb Bb | C C C C | D —→ C —→ | Bb —→ – – |
1 2 3 4 1 2 3 4 1 2 3 4 1 2 3 4 1 2 3 4 1 2 3 4 1 2 3 4 1 2 3 4

MARY HAD A LITTLE LAMB
D C Bb C | D D D – | C C C – | D D D – | D C Bb C | D D D – | C C D C | Bb —→ – – |
1 2 3 4 1 2 3 4 1 2 3 4 1 2 3 4 1 2 3 4 1 2 3 4 1 2 3 4 1 2 3 4

COMPOSER'S CORNER

It is your turn to compose your *own* piece of music! Use the three notes you know to complete this piece.
Give it a title and perform it for a friend or family member!

Title: _Super bar_   Composer (your name):  _Max G_

Bb D D C | B – B – | B C B – | D C Bb – |

 # OPUS 1

 THEORY

MUSIC STAFF
The **music staff** is where notes and rests are written. It has 5 lines and 4 spaces.

LONG TONE
A **long tone** is a held note. The fermata (⌢) indicates to hold the note until your teacher tells you to rest.

measures

BAR LINES
Bar lines divide the music staff into measures.

FINAL BAR LINE
A **final bar** line indicates the end of a piece.

1.1 FIRST NOTE *Practice each long tone daily to improve your sound!*

 TRACK 1 2

 NEW NOTE!
D
(4th position)

final bar line

 RHYTHM

BEAT
The **beat** is the pulse of the music. Tap your foot to keep a steady beat!

1 2 3 4

NOTES AND RESTS
Notes represent sound. **Rests** represent silence.

Quarter Note = 1 beat of sound

Quarter Rest = 1 beat of silence

1.2 FOUR IN A ROW *This piece has four beats in each measure. Remember to tap your foot.*

 TRACK 1 3

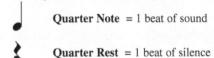

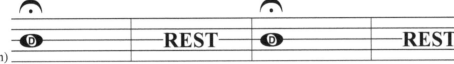

1 2 3 4   1 2 3 4   1 2 3 4   1 2 3 4   1 2 3 4

1.3 SECOND NOTE

TRACK 1 4

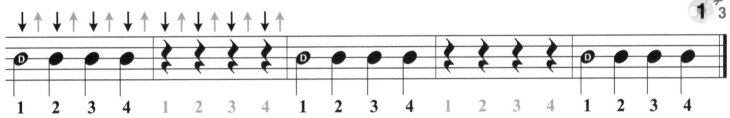

 NEW NOTE!
C
(6th position)

1.4 FOUR MORE *How many measures do you see?*

TRACK 1 5

1 2 3 4   1 2 3 4   1 2 3 4   1 2 3 4   1 2 3 4

1.5 UP AND DOWN *Any time you see a Bonus Box, write in the note name.*

TRACK 1 6

 BONUS BOX

1.6 ALL MIXED UP

TRACK 1 7

 BONUS BOX

ACCIDENTALS

Accidentals are signs that alter a note's pitch. They are placed to the left of the note.

Flat (♭) A flat sign lowers the pitch by one half-step. This pitch remains lowered for the rest of the measure.

Sharp (♯) A sharp sign raises the pitch by one half-step. This pitch remains raised for the rest of the measure.

Natural (♮) A natural sign cancels a flat or sharp. It remains cancelled for the rest of the measure.

1.7 THIRD NOTE'S A CHARM

1.8 ALL TOGETHER

1.9 WHAT GOES UP...

1.10 RHYTHM RENDEZVOUS

CLEFS

Clefs are signs that help name notes.

The **bass clef**, also called the **F clef**, names F on the bass staff. The two dots appear on both sides of 4th line F. The musical alphabet uses A B C D E F and G. Each line and space of the staff has a note name. To find a bass clef note, move up or down by lines and spaces in the musical alphabet sequence.

LEDGER LINES

Ledger lines extend the staff. Notes written above or below the staff appear with ledger lines.

NAME THAT NOTE... *Use your knowledge of the musical alphabet to fill in the Bonus Boxes!*

HALF NOTES AND WHOLE NOTES

Half Note
2 beats of sound

Whole Note
4 beats of sound

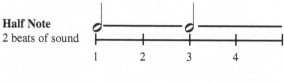

HALF RESTS AND WHOLE RESTS

Half Rest
2 beats of silence
(sits on a line)

Whole Rest
4 beats of silence
(hangs from a line)

TIME SIGNATURE

The top number shows the number of beats in each measure.
The bottom number shows the type of note that receives one beat.
*Hint: Replace the top number with a "1" and you will get a
fraction that equals the type of note that gets one beat!*

Number of beats in a measure
Type of note that gets one beat

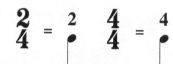

1.11 GOING PLACES *Circle the half rests.*

time signature

1 2 3 4   1 2 3 4   1 2 3 4   1 2 3 4   1 2 3 4   1 2 3 4   1 2 3 4   1 2 3 4

THEORY

FERMATA

When playing on your own, hold a note with a
fermata longer than its assigned value.

1.12 COUNTDOWN *Hold the note with a fermata longer than its assigned value.*

fermata

1 2 3 4   1 2 3 4

THEORY

REPEAT SIGN

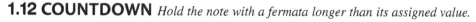

A **repeat sign** is a final bar line with two dots.
Without stopping, go back to the beginning
and play the music a second time.

1.13 TURN AROUND *Say the note names and demonstrate your slide positions before you play.*

repeat sign

1.14 HOT CROSS BUNS

English Folk Song

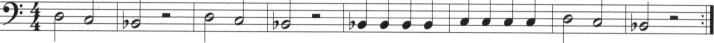

1.15 HERE WE GO! *Draw in the bar lines, then play!*

BONUS BOX

BB208TBN

1.16 AU CLAIRE DE LA LUNE *Musicianship Challenge! – Without the CD, play 1ˢᵗ time quietly, 2ⁿᵈ time loudly.* French Folk Song

1.17 MARY HAD A LITTLE LAMB Traditional

1.18 MARY HAD A COOL LAMB Traditional Melody

STYLE AND FORM: DUET

A **duet** has two different parts performed simultaneously by two individuals or groups.

1.19 BEAT STREET — Duet *A Beat Street exercise indicates to clap the rhythm.*

1.20 DUET LIKE THIS

1.21 CLIMBING HIGHER

NEW NOTE! E♭

1.22 HOME BASE

1.23 EVEN HIGHER! *Trace the clef!*

NEW NOTE! F

THEORY

PHRASING

A **phrase** in music is similar to a sentence in speech. It should continue uninterrupted until the music indicates a breath.

, A **breath mark** indicates to take a breath through your mouth.

1.24 DOWN BY THE STATION

American Folk Song

TRACK 1 25

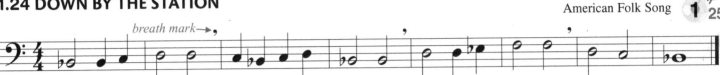

HISTORY

MUSIC
Stephen Collins Foster (1826 – 1864) was an American songwriter born in Pennsylvania. He published his first piece when he was 18 years old. Some of his most famous songs are *Oh! Susanna, Camptown Races,* and *Some Folks Do.* His compositions capture the spirit of American folk music during the 1800s.

ART
During this time in history, artists of the Hudson River School were hard at work in the United States. Frederic Church painted *Morning, Looking East Over the Hudson Valley from the Catskill Mountains* about the same time that *Camptown Races* was written.

WORLD
The world was introduced to Ebenezer Scrooge (the famous character in Charles Dickens' *A Christmas Carol*), Abraham Lincoln delivered the Gettysburg Address, and the stapler was patented.

1.25 SOME FOLKS DO
Before you play, draw these symbols where they belong: Bass Clef, Time Signature, Final Bar Line.

Stephen C. Foster

TRACK 1 26

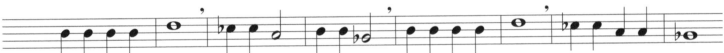

1.26 SCALING THE WALL *Work with another student to learn this piece.*

TRACK 1 27

BONUS BOX

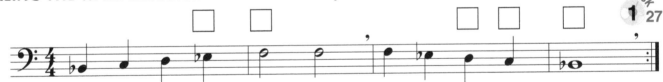

ON THE PODIUM

CONDUCTING IN $\frac{4}{4}$ TIME

Your band director has been conducting a four-beat pattern. Now it is your turn to conduct! Place your right hand in a "handshake" position and follow the diagram to conduct in $\frac{4}{4}$ time.

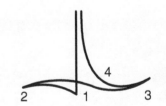

1.27 GOOD KING WENCESLAS *Conduct a partner, your section, or the entire class!*

English Carol

TRACK 1 28

ON THE PODIUM

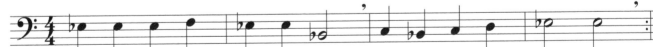

1.28 STOMP ROCK

TRACK 1 29

stomp

INTERPRETATION STATION

Listen to CD 1 Track 30. Describe the music and how it makes you feel.

SIMON "SEZ"

Your director will give you a starting note. Listen to the rhythms your director plays and echo them back. Listen carefully!

COMPOSER'S CORNER

A composer is someone who creates original music. It is YOUR turn to be a composer!
Using the notes you already know, complete this composition. Guide rhythms have been provided for you in parentheses.

Title:_____ Name:_____

PENCIL POWER

Match the following terms with their symbols.

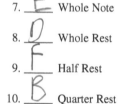

1. I Clef
2. C Time Signature
3. A Repeat Sign
4. G Fermata
5. H Half Note

6. J Quarter Note
7. E Whole Note
8. D Whole Rest
9. F Half Rest
10. B Quarter Rest

A: :| B: 𝄽   C: 4/4   D: ▬

E: 𝅝   F: ▬   G: 𝄐   H: 𝅗𝅥

I: 𝄢   J: 𝅘𝅥

CURTAIN UP!

Time to perform! Practice these pieces and play them for friends or family members. Introduce each piece by its title.
Remember to bow when you are finished!

1.29 GO TELL AUNT RHODY *Teach your audience to conduct a four-beat pattern!*

American Folk Song

ON THE PODIUM

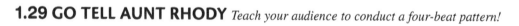

1.30 CUCKOO SAMBA

1.31 LIGHTLY ROW — Duet *Pair up with a friend to perform this piece for your audience.*
Switch parts on the repeat!

Traditional

☀ OPUS 2

HISTORY

MUSIC

Ludwig van Beethoven (1770 – 1827) lived most of his life in Vienna, Austria. His music became a bridge between Classical and Romantic music. When *Symphony No. 9* and its *Ode to Joy* were performed for the first time, Beethoven was completely deaf!

ART

Romanticism in art was an important movement in Europe and themes often included nationalism. Eugene Delacroix was one of the most important French artists. His *Liberty Leading the People* commemorates the French Revolution of 1830 and the overthrow of King Charles X.

WORLD

Around this time in history, Mexico became a republic, trains first carried passengers in England, the first photograph was taken, and ice cream was first sold in the United States!

2.1 ODE TO JOY *Musicianship Challenge! – Without the CD, play the 1ˢᵗ phrase gently, the 2ⁿᵈ phrase majestically.*

Ludwig van Beethoven — TRACK 1 · 34

2.2 OUTER LIMITS

NEW NOTE! **G**

TRACK 1 · 35

2.3 OLD MACDONALD

American Folk Song — TRACK 1 · 36

continue to the next line

2.4 SHARK! *Musicianship Challenge! – Without the CD, play this like you are being chased.*

NEW NOTE! **A**

TRACK 1 · 37

Choose any note you have learned!

2.5 CRUSADER'S HYMN *Play each phrase in one breath.*

Silesian Folk Song — TRACK 1 · 38

THEORY

KEY SIGNATURE

The **key signature** indicates which notes to play sharp or flat. It appears at the beginning of each staff.

This is the key of B♭ **Major.**

- There can be up to 7 sharps in a key signature. **Sharps** (♯) follow this order: F, C, G, D, A, E, B
- There can be up to 7 flats in a key signature. **Flats** (♭) follow this order: B, E, A, D, G, C, F
- Your key signature in 2.6, *Keynote March*, indicates that all Bs and Es should be played as B-flats and E-flats.

2.6 KEYNOTE MARCH *Musicianship Challenge! – Play this piece like you would hear it in a parade.*

TRACK 1 · 39

key signature

BB208TBN

MUSIC

Wolfgang Amadeus Mozart (1756 – 1791) was born in Salzburg, Austria. He was a child genius and composed his first minuet when he was just five years old! During his short life of 35 years, he wrote over 600 musical compositions. Many of his works continue to be performed today.

ART

As Mozart wrote in the Classical style, Neoclassicism in visual art was being explored by artists such as Jacques-Louis David, a French painter. This style can be seen in his painting, *The Death of Socrates,* which was completed in 1787.

WORLD

The thirteen American Colonies broke away from the British Empire in the American Revolutionary War, the *Declaration of Independence* was signed, and Johnny Appleseed was born.

2.7 STAR SEARCH *This piece is in the key of _____ Major.*

French Melody
adapted by Wolfgang A. Mozart

TRACK 1 40

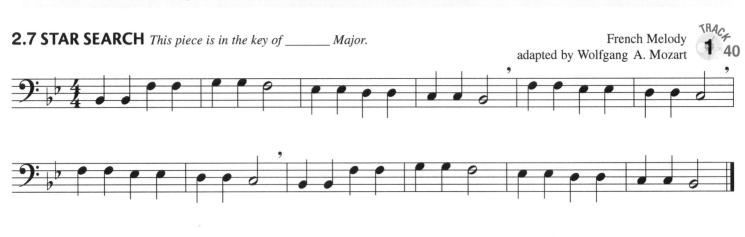

THEORY

DYNAMICS

Dynamics indicate how loudly or softly to play. Italian terms are often used in music to indicate volume.

p (*piano*) – play softly   ***f*** (*forte*) – play loudly

2.8 BEAT STREET *Clap the rhythm with dynamics!*

TRACK 1 41

CLAP

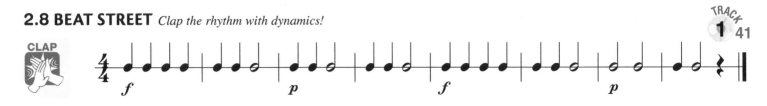

2.9 LONDON BRIDGE *Show phrasing by placing breath marks in this piece before you play it.*

English Folk Song

TRACK 1 42

2.10 JINGLE BELLS – Duet

James Pierpont

TRACK 1 43

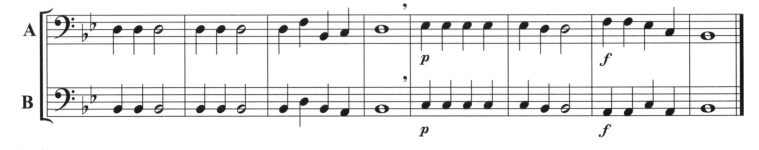

ON THE PODIUM

When dynamics indicate *loud*, a conductor's gestures are bigger.
When dynamics indicate *soft*, gestures are smaller.
Practice conducting a four-beat pattern with dynamics!

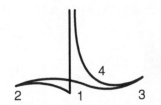

2.11 DREIDEL SONG

Traditional Hannukah Song

TRACK 1 44

DYNAMICS

Mezzo is an Italian term that means "medium" or "moderately." The letter *m* is an abbreviation used in dynamics.

mp (*mezzo piano*) – play moderately soft   *mf* (*mezzo forte*) – play moderately loud

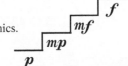

2.12 BEAT STREET *Clap the dynamics!*

TRACK 1 45

2.13 DYNAMIC DOODLE ALL DAY

American Folk Melody

TRACK 1 46

PICK-UP NOTES

Pick-up notes lead into the first full measure of a phrase.
When pick-up notes are used to begin a piece, their combined rhythmic value is often subtracted from the last measure.

2.14 A–TISKET, A–TASKET

American Folk Song

TRACK 1 47

2.15 OH! SUSANNA – Duet

Stephen C. Foster

TRACK 1 48

14

2.16 AFRICAN SAFARI

 NEW NOTE! G

p   mp   mf   f

 **THEORY**

ARTICULATION: ACCENT

> An **accent** indicates to emphasize a note by playing louder. Use your air!

2.17 LEAN ON IT

mf

2.18 WALK TO MY LOU

American Folk Melody

 RHYTHM

SYNCOPATION

Music has strong beats and weak beats. Most of the time, we stress strong beats (**1** 2 **3** 4).
Sometimes, we shift the stress onto weak beats (1 **2** 3 **4**).
This is known as **syncopation**. Longer, accented notes that occur on weak beats often identify syncopation.

2.19 BEAT STREET

CLAP

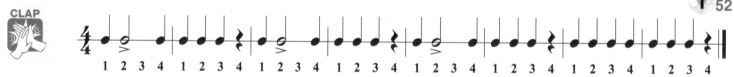

1 2 3 4   1 2 3 4   1 2 3 4   1 2 3 4   1 2 3 4   1 2 3 4   1 2 3 4   1 2 3 4

2.20 SHOO FLY

American Folk Song

1 2 3 4   1 2 3 4   1 2 3 4   1 2 3 4   1 2 3 4   1 2 3 4   1 2 3 4   1 2 3 4

2.21 CHANT

mp

 BB208TBN

OPUS 2 ENCORE!

INTERPRETATION STATION

Listen to CD 1 Track 55. You will hear two performances of the same piece. Which one is more musical and why?

SIMON "SEZ"

Listen to CD 1 Track 56. You will hear a well-known song. Listen first, sing it, then find the pitches on your instrument. You can then play along with the accompaniment track that follows. Can you match the initial recording?

COMPOSER'S CORNER

Use the notes and rhythms you have learned to complete the composition. Be sure to give it a title!

Title:_____   Name:_____

PENCIL POWER

The Secret Decoder: Name the notes and solve the puzzles!

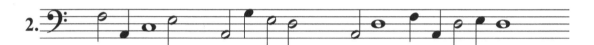

Beethoven went ___ ___ ___ ___ towards the end of his life.

The ___ ___ ___ ___ in the ___ ___ ___ ___ photo h___ ___ ___ ___ ___ ___ with time.

H___ h___ ___ to pay an extra ___ ___ ___ for the ___ i ___ ___ ___ ___ ___ ___ .

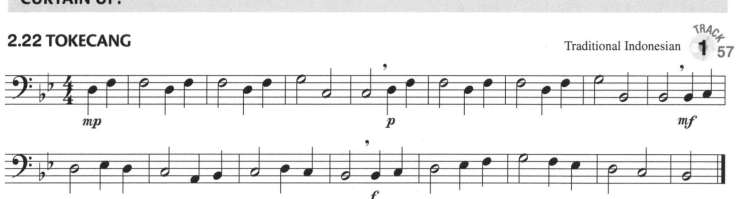

He ___ ___ ___ ___ ___ ___ when he mistakenly ate ___ ___ ___ corned ___ ___ ___ ___ and ___ ___ ___ ___ ___ ___ ___ !

CURTAIN UP!

2.22 TOKECANG

Traditional Indonesian

CURTAIN UP! FIRST CONCERT

2.23 CONCERT WARM–UP NO. 1

TRACK 1 58

2.24 CONCERT WARM–UP NO. 2

TRACK 1 59

2.25 THE SYNCOPATED ROW BOAT – Duet

Traditional Melody

TRACK 1 60

2.26 CROWN OF MAJESTY – Full Band

Robert Sheldon

TRACK 1 61

9 ← *rehearsal number*

2.27 OBWISANA – Duet or Full Band with Percussion

Ghanian Folk Song

TRACK 1 62

2.28 FANFARE FOR A WINTER CELEBRATION – Full Band

arr. Brian Balmages

TRACK 1 63

2.29 THE SECTION BATTLE RAG – Full Band

To play a glissando, tongue the first note, then move the slide without tonguing.

Brian Balmages

TRACK 1 64

16 Section Feature!
Circle the measure(s) your director asks you to play! ⌐ – – – – – – – – – – – – – – ¬ tutti (everyone)

2.30 ON CARIBBEAN SHORES (MARY ANN) – Full Band

Jamaican Folk Song
arr. Robert Sheldon

TRACK 1 65

2.31 ROCK THE HOUSE – Full Band

Brian Balmages

TRACK 1 66

✳ OPUS 3

MORE TIME SIGNATURES

3/4 **3 beats** in each measure
Quarter note gets one beat

2/4 **2 beats** in each measure
Quarter note gets one beat

3.1 BEAT STREET

TRACK 1 67

3.2 THREE'S A CROWD

TRACK 1 68

3.3 THREE POINTER

TRACK 1 69

3.4 BEAT STREET

TRACK 1 70

3.5 RAIN, RAIN, GO AWAY

Traditional   TRACK 1 71

ON THE PODIUM

CONDUCTING IN 2/4 TIME

It is your turn to conduct a two-beat pattern.
With your right hand in a "handshake" position,
follow the diagram to conduct in 2/4 time.

3.6 TWO FOR YOU

ON THE PODIUM

TRACK 1 72

3.7 TERRIBLE TWOS

TRACK 1 73

REVISITING ACCIDENTALS

Accidentals include **flat** (♭), **sharp** (♯), and **natural** (♮) signs found in front of notes, but not in the key signature.
A flat sign (♭) lowers the pitch one half-step. It remains in effect for the rest of the measure.

3.8 CANYONS

NEW KEY SIGNATURE

This is the key of E♭ **Major.**

This key signature indicates that all Bs, Es, and As should be played as B-flats, E-flats, and A-flats.

3.9 ROYAL SCEPTER *Musicianship Challenge! – Play this piece in a noble style.*

3.10 THINGS ARE LOOKING UP *Add a breath mark after the first phrase.*

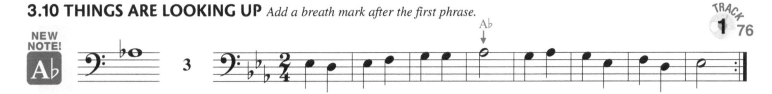

THE RULE OF THE DOT

Adding a dot after a note increases the length of the note *by half its value.*
When adding a dot to a half note, it becomes a **dotted half note.**

2 beats + 1 beat = 3 beats   2 beats + 1 beat = 3 beats

3.11 BEAT STREET

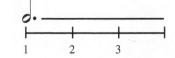

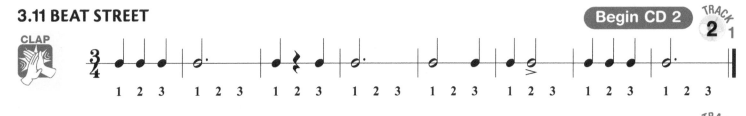

3.12 TRIPLE CROWN

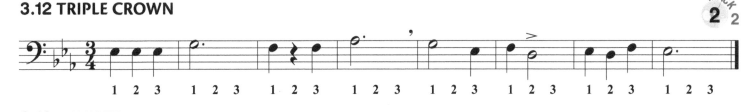

3.13 MINUET

Daniel G. Türk

BB208TBN

3.21 SKIP TO MY LOU

American Folk Song · TRACK 2 · 11

WHOLE MEASURE REST

Rest for the entire measure. Check the time signature!

3.22 WALTZING LOU *How should you play these dynamics?*

American Folk Melody · TRACK 2 · 12

(1 - 2 - 3)

THEORY

ENCLOSED REPEAT SIGNS

Repeat the music between the two signs.

3.23 TWO BY FOUR

TRACK 2 · 13

THEORY

STYLE AND FORM: ROUND

In a **round**, each musician plays the same part, but enters at a different time.

3.24 FRÉRE JACQUES – Round *As each musician reaches ② , the next musician should begin playing at ① .*

French Folk Song · TRACK 2 · 14

THEORY

STYLE AND FORM: THEME AND VARIATIONS

Composers create a **variation** when they change a melody in some way. Changes can be made to the notes, rhythm, key, and even the time signature! While you will notice the differences in each variation, you will still be able to recognize the original theme.

A **double bar line** indicates the end of one section and the beginning of another.

3.25 VARIATIONS ON A FRENCH MELODY

TRACK 2 · 15

Theme ... **Variation 1**

Variation 2

BB208TBN

THEORY

DYNAMICS

Crescendo means to gradually play louder.

Decrescendo means to gradually play softer.

3.26 IT'S SWELL *Clap first, then play!*
TRACK 2 16

3.27 OUTTA MY WAY
TRACK 2 17

3.28 REGAL FANFARE
TRACK 2 18

HISTORY

MUSIC
German born **George Frideric Handel** (1685 – 1759) composed many types of music including oratorios, operas, and orchestral works. *Music for the Royal Fireworks* was written when George II of Great Britain hired him to write music to accompany fireworks in London. The event commemorated the signing of the Treaty of Aix-la-Chapelle in 1749.

ART
During colonial times, American painting and drawing focused on portraiture. Joseph Badger painted portraits of prominent figures and children in colonial Boston. His style can be seen in the portrait of *Jeremiah Belknap*, painted in 1758.

WORLD
Sir Isaac Newton stated the three universal laws of motion. In the same publication he used the Latin word *gravitas* that would become known as gravity. Also, America founded its first hospital in Pennsylvania.

3.29 MUSIC FOR THE ROYAL FIREWORKS
George F. Handel
TRACK 2 19

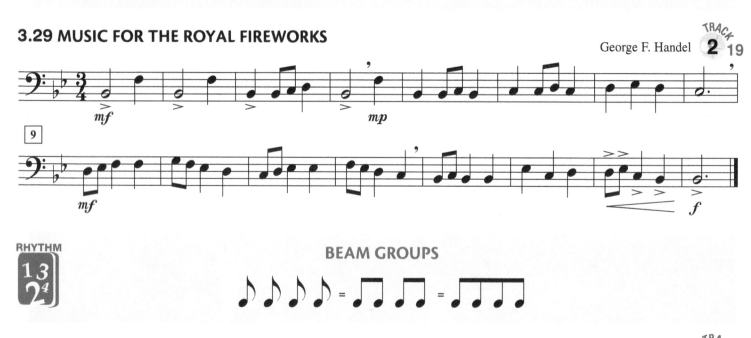

RHYTHM

BEAM GROUPS

3.30 SCALE THE WALL
TRACK 2 20

3.31 NEW FRONTIERS

NEW NOTE! B♭

TRACK **2** 21

3.32 THE SAINTS GO MARCHING IN *Pick-up notes lead into measure 1.*

pick-up notes **1**

Traditional Spiritual   TRACK **2** 22

9

ON THE PODIUM

CONDUCTING IN 3/4 TIME

It is your turn to conduct a three-beat pattern. With your right hand in a "handshake" position, follow the diagram to conduct in 3/4 time.

3.33 ROLLING ALONG

ON THE PODIUM

TRACK **2** 23

THEORY

FIRST AND SECOND ENDINGS

At the **first ending**, play through it to the repeat sign. Go back to the beginning or the previous repeat sign and play again. Skip the first ending – play the **second ending** instead.

1.   **2.**

second time

3.34 LONG, LONG AGO

Traditional   TRACK **2** 24

1.   **2.**

3.35 JOLLY OLD SAINT NICHOLAS – Duet

American Carol   TRACK **2** 25

A

B

1.   **2.**

OPUS 3 ENCORE!

INTERPRETATION STATION

TRACK 2 26

Listen to CD 2 Track 26. You will hear four musical examples, all composed using a different time signature.
As you listen, pay close attention to how rhythmic ideas are grouped. Circle the correct time signature for each example.

1. $\frac{3}{4}$ $\frac{4}{4}$ 2. $\frac{2}{4}$ $\frac{3}{4}$ 3. $\frac{3}{4}$ $\frac{4}{4}$ 4. $\frac{2}{4}$ $\frac{3}{4}$

SIMON "SEZ"

TRACK 2 27

Listen to CD 2 Track 27. You are going to hear a piece called *One Note Wonder*. It gets its title because it uses only one pitch!
You will hear dynamics that make it very interesting. Play along with the accompaniment track that follows, imitating the dynamics
and rhythm of the initial recording to make it musical.

COMPOSER'S CORNER

It is your turn to be a composer again! Use notes and rhythms you have learned to complete each measure (remember to
look at the time signature). Then give your piece a title and perform it for a friend or family member!

Title:_____   Name:_____

PENCIL POWER

Each measure below is rhythmically incomplete! For each example, add *one note* to complete the measure and make it correct.

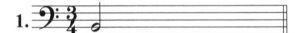   

   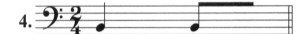

CURTAIN UP!

3.36 ZUM GALI GALI – Round

Traditional Hebrew Song   TRACK 2 28

3.37 DRY BONES

Spiritual   TRACK 2 29

CURTAIN UP!

MULTIPLE MEASURE REST

In some pieces, there will be instances when you rest for a few measures at a time. When this happens, you will see the **multiple measure rest** symbol. The number above the symbol tells you how many measures of rest to count.

Count: **1** 2 3 4 | **2** 2 3 4   **1** 2 3 | **2** 2 3 | **3** 2 3

This symbol tells you to rest for two measures in $\frac{4}{4}$ time.   This symbol tells you to rest for three measures in $\frac{3}{4}$ time.

3.38 WILLIAM TELL OVERTURE

Gioachino Rossini
arr. Brian Balmages

TRACK 2 · 30

3.39 ABOVE THE CLOUDS

Robert Sheldon

TRACK 2 · 31

✳ OPUS 4

4.1 CIRCUS ACT

NEW NOTE! **E**

4.2 DAYBREAK

ON THE PODIUM

Legato *(smooth and flowing)*

THEORY

NEW KEY SIGNATURE

This is the key of **F Major.**

This key signature indicates that all Bs should be played as B-flats.

4.3 CHIAPANECAS

BONUS BOX

new key signature

Mexican Folk Song

stomp

THEORY

ARTICULATION: SLUR

A **slur** is a curved line that connects notes of *different* pitches. Tongue the first note of a slur normally. Use a "dah" articulation for the other notes connected by a slur to achieve a smooth legato sound.

4.4 SLURRED NOT SHAKEN

NEW NOTE! **A**

Legato

4.5 SLIP 'N' SLIDE

TEMPO

Tempo is the speed of the beat. Music can move at different rates of speed.

Largo – a slow tempo   **Moderato** – a medium tempo   **Allegro** – a fast tempo

4.6 MUSETTE

J.S. Bach

TRACK 2 37

Moderato

mf

4.7 CIELITO LINDO

Mexican Folk Song

TRACK 2 38

ON THE PODIUM

Allegro

f

HISTORY

MUSIC

Gustav Mahler (1860 – 1911) was a noted composer and conductor of the late Romantic era. He spent time in New York conducting the Metropolitan Opera and the New York Philharmonic Orchestra. He is mainly known for his large symphonies (his *Symphony No. 8* uses over a thousand performers!).

ART

The world saw the emergence of Cubism, a style in which objects were broken up, then reassembled in abstract forms. Pablo Picasso became one of the most famous Cubists in history. His *Ma Jolie* (1911) is an early example of the style.

WORLD

Mark Twain published *The Adventures of Tom Sawyer*, Sir Arthur Conan Doyle introduced the world to Sherlock Holmes, and the coin-operated telephone was invented.

4.8 THEME FROM SYMPHONY NO. 1 – Round

Gustav Mahler

TRACK 2 39

Largo

mp

mf   *p*

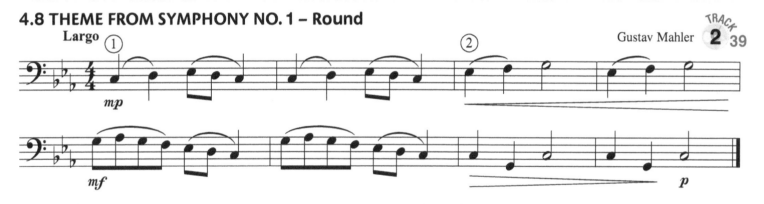

RHYTHM

TIE

A **tie** is a curved line that connects notes of the *same* pitch. These notes are "tied" together and played to sound like one longer note.

4.9 MAKING CONNECTIONS

TRACK 2 40

mp   *f*   *mp*

4.10 ALL TIED UP

TRACK 2 41

mf - f

HISTORY

MUSIC

Pyotr Ilyich Tchaikovsky (1840 – 1893) was a Russian composer who studied music at a very young age. His most famous works include the ballet *The Nutcracker* and the exciting *1812 Overture*. He composed *Capriccio Italien* after a visit to Italy during Carnivale season.

ART

In 1880, the Arts and Crafts Movement was going strong in England. This style is reflected in art, architecture, and interior design. Works by British architect Herbert Tudor Buckland and American architect Frank Lloyd Wright are typical of the Arts and Crafts style.

WORLD

Wabash, Indiana became the first town to be completely illuminated using electric light and the Statue of Liberty was presented to the United States by the people of France.

4.11 CAPRICCIO ITALIEN *How many slurs are in this piece?*

Pyotr I. Tchaikovsky · TRACK 2 42

Allegro

4.12 BARCAROLLE

Jacques Offenbach · TRACK 2 43

NEW NOTE!
Db

NEW KEY SIGNATURE

THEORY

This is the key of A♭ **Major.**

This key signature indicates that all Bs, Es, As, and Ds should be played as B-flats, E-flats, A-flats, and D-flats.

4.13 THE BLUE BELLS OF SCOTLAND

Scottish Folk Song · TRACK 2 44

Maestoso *(majestically)*

HISTORY

MUSIC

John Philip Sousa (1854 – 1932) was a violinist, composer, and conductor born in Washington, D.C. He conducted the United States Marine Band from 1880 until 1892. His marches, such as *The Stars and Stripes Forever, Semper Fidelis*, and the *Liberty Bell*, are well known and important to American culture.

ART

In the early 20th century, artist Salvador Dali of Spain was mostly known as a surrealist and emphasized visions of the subconscious. *The Persistence of Memory* (1931), a scene with melting clocks, is one of his best known works.

WORLD

Elsewhere in 1917, the Russian revolution began, World War I was still raging, and the first commercial recordings of jazz music were available to the public.

4.14 HIGH SCHOOL CADETS

John Philip Sousa · TRACK 2 45

March tempo

4.15 IT'S ONLY NATURAL

TRACK 2 46

BONUS BOX

Dolce *(sweetly)*

4.16 ACCIDENTAL BLUES – Duet

TRACK 2 47

courtesy accidental

RETURN OF THE DOT RULE

RHYTHM 13 2 4

Adding a dot after a note increases the length of the note by half its value. Here, the dot is used with a quarter note to create a **dotted quarter note**.

4.17 BEAT STREET *Tap your foot to keep a steady beat.*

TRACK 2 48

CLAP

1 + 2 + 3 + 4 +   1 + 2 + 3 + 4 +   1 + 2 + 3 + 4 +   1 + 2 + 3 + 4 +

4.18 DOTS A LOT

TRACK 2 49

1 + 2 + 3 + 4 +   1 + 2 + 3 + 4 +   1 + 2 + 3 + 4 +   1 + 2 + 3 + 4 +

RITARDANDO

THEORY

Ritardando – abbreviated "*rit.*" – means to make the tempo gradually slower.

4.19 ALL THROUGH THE NIGHT

Welsh Folk Song

TRACK 2 50

BONUS BOX

Dolce

1.   2. *rit.*

p - mp

4.20 AMERICA

Maestoso

Traditional

TRACK 2 51

 THEORY

D.C. AL FINE

D.C. is an abbreviation for *da capo*, an Italian term that refers to the beginning.
At the **D.C. al Fine**, return to the beginning and play again until the **Fine**.

4.21 ALOUETTE

French-Canadian Folk Song

TRACK 2 52

Moderato

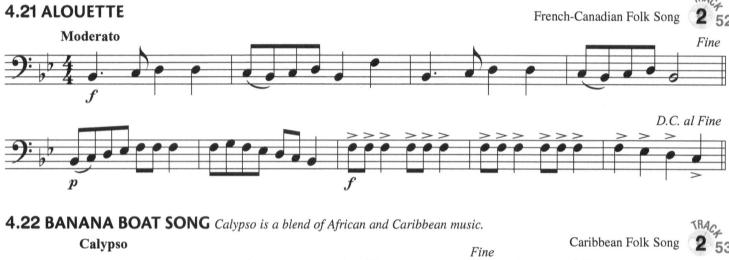

4.22 BANANA BOAT SONG *Calypso is a blend of African and Caribbean music.*

Calypso

Caribbean Folk Song

TRACK 2 53

 HISTORY

MUSIC

Antonín Dvořák (1841 – 1904) was from a small town near Prague, in the Czech Republic. He eventually moved to the United States and became the director of the New York Conservatory of Music. In 1888, the Conservatory welcomed African-Americans while other schools were still practicing segregation. His *Symphony No. 9 ("From the New World")* was composed during his brief time in America. It is influenced by Native American music and African-American spirituals.

ART

French artist Georges Seurat painted *A Sunday Afternoon on the Island of La Grande Jatte*. This large painting, depicting a scene of recreation in Paris, was created using a technique called pointillism. Composed entirely of painted dots, it took him nearly two years to finish.

WORLD

Congress abolished slavery in the U.S. Territories, Albert Einstein was born, the World's Columbian Exposition was held in Chicago, and New York became the first state to require license plates on cars.

4.23 THEME FROM THE NEW WORLD SYMPHONY

Largo

Antonín Dvořák

TRACK 2 54

MORE ABOUT THE DOT

While a dotted quarter note is usually followed by an eighth note, the eighth note sometimes appears *before* the dotted quarter note.

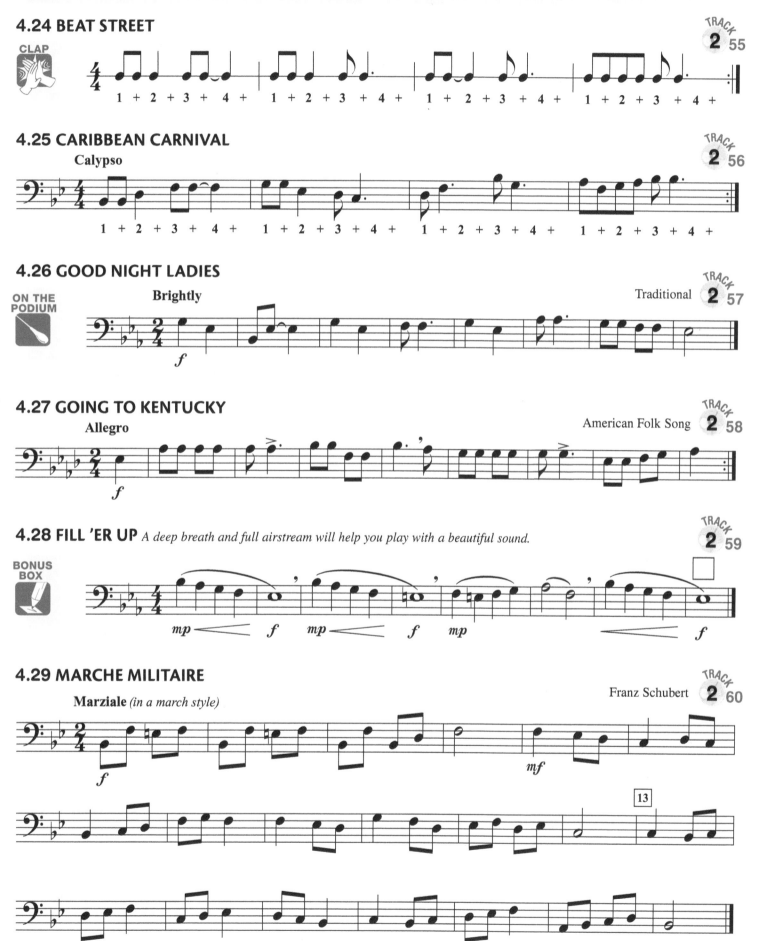

4.24 BEAT STREET

4.25 CARIBBEAN CARNIVAL

Calypso

4.26 GOOD NIGHT LADIES

Brightly   Traditional

4.27 GOING TO KENTUCKY

Allegro   American Folk Song

4.28 FILL 'ER UP *A deep breath and full airstream will help you play with a beautiful sound.*

4.29 MARCHE MILITAIRE

Marziale *(in a march style)*   Franz Schubert

OPUS 4 ENCORE!

INTERPRETATION STATION

Listen to CD 2 Track 61. For each example, decide if the tempo is *Largo, Moderato,* or *Allegro.*
Circle the correct answer.

1. L M A   2. L M A   3. L M A   4. L M A

SIMON "SEZ"

Listen to CD 2 Track 62. You are going to hear the same five-note pattern articulated four different ways.
Match the performance to its correctly notated example. The first one has been done for you!

No. 1 = __B__   No. 2 = _____   No. 3 = _____   No. 4 = _____

COMPOSER'S CORNER

Sometimes a composer takes an existing melody and presents it in a new way. This is called **arranging**. Change the rhythms of the music in *Alouette in Four* so it is playable in $\frac{2}{4}$ time. *Hint: Cut the rhythmic value of each note in half!* The arrangement has been started for you.

ALOUETTE IN FOUR

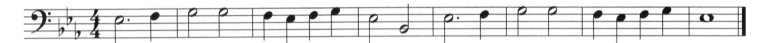

ALOUETTE IN TWO

PENCIL POWER – MATCH THE COMPOSER

Match the composer with the correct fact by writing in the appropriate letter.

_____ Wolfgang Amadeus Mozart

_____ Antonín Dvořák

_____ Gustav Mahler

_____ John Philip Sousa

_____ Ludwig van Beethoven

_____ Pyotr Ilyich Tchaikovsky

A.   Russian composer who wrote the famous ballet, *The Nutcracker*

B.   U.S. Marine Band conductor and composer known for his marches

C.   His *Symphony No. 9* reveals the influence of African-American spirituals

D.   Child genius who composed over 600 works in a short life of 35 years

E.   Continued to compose music after becoming completely deaf

F.   Composer of the late Romantic era known for his large symphonies

CURTAIN UP!

4.30 HAVA NASHIRA – Round

Israeli Folk Song

CURTAIN UP!

4.31 LITTLE SWALLOW

Chinese Folk Song
arr. Robert Sheldon

TRACK 2 64

4.32 FURY *divisi (div.) – Part of the section plays the top note and part of the section plays the bottom note.*

Brian Balmages

TRACK 2 65

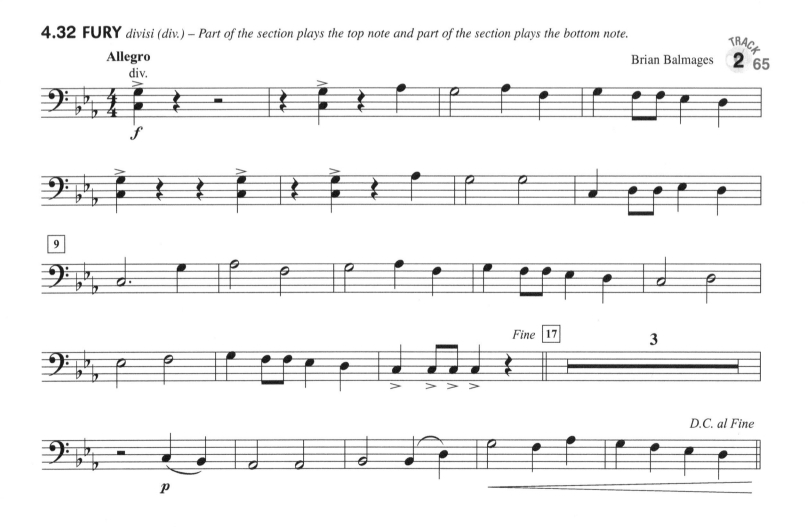

BB208TBN

4.33 HAIL THE CONQUERING HERO
Instrumental Solo

George F. Handel
arr. Brian Balmages

BB208TBN

✳ OPUS 5

In this Opus, all brass players focus on lip slurs (slurring between two different notes that use the same slide position).
Use a full and steady air stream.

5.1 CATAPULT!

Begin CD 3 — TRACK 3 1

5.2 UP AND OVER

TRACK 3 2

5.3 SMOOTH HORIZONS
Sometimes it is better to use an alternate slide position to make technique smoother.
Alternate F is particularly useful when approaching or leaving low C.

TRACK 3 3

use alt. F throughout

5.4 UP, UP AND AWAY!

TRACK 3 4

5.5 CLIMB ON

TRACK 3 5

5.6 OVER EASY

TRACK 3 6

5.7 ZERO GRAVITY

TRACK 3 7

5.8 BREAKING THROUGH

TRACK 3 8

5.9 THE MOON TURNS DARK

French Folk Melody

TRACK 3 9

Misterioso *(mysteriously)*

BB208TBN

37

HISTORY

MUSIC

German composer **Johannes Brahms** (1833 – 1897) was also an accomplished pianist and gave the first performance of many of his own works. *Lullaby (Wiegenlied)* was composed in 1868 to celebrate the birth of his friend's son.

ART

In the mid 1800s, Realists were concerned with objectivity. American artist James Whistler titled many of his works "harmonies" or "arrangements." An example is his *Arrangement in Grey and Black No. 1: Portrait of the Artist's Mother.*

WORLD

In 1868, floats appeared in New Orleans' Mardi Gras parade for the first time and the first Memorial Day was celebrated in the United States.

5.17 LULLABY – Duet

Cantabile *(in a singing style)*

Johannes Brahms — TRACK 3 17

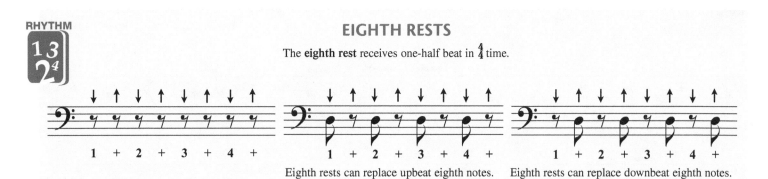

RHYTHM

EIGHTH RESTS

The **eighth rest** receives one-half beat in $\frac{4}{4}$ time.

Eighth rests can replace upbeat eighth notes.

Eighth rests can replace downbeat eighth notes.

5.18 BEAT STREET

TRACK 3 18

CLAP

5.19 SCALING WITH EIGHTH RESTS

TRACK 3 19

HISTORY

MUSIC

German composer **Johann Sebastian Bach** (1685 – 1750) began learning music as a young boy, studying violin and organ. He is thought to be one of the greatest composers who ever lived. His work is the model of the Baroque style.

ART

Peter Paul Rubens painted a series of works in the Baroque Style for Marie de Medici at the Luxembourg Palace in Paris, France. These works are now on display at the Louvre, one of the most famous art museums in the world.

WORLD

The tuning fork was invented by Englishman John Shore, the first folding umbrella was manufactured in France, and infamous pirate Edward Teach (Blackbeard) terrorized people along the Atlantic coast.

5.20 MINUET NO. 1

Moderato

J. S. Bach — TRACK 3 20

5.21 BEAT STREET

5.22 STEPPIN' OFF THE EIGHTH

5.23 TIPTOE TANGO *Tango is a type of music and dance that originated in Buenos Aires, Argentina.*

5.24 ROCK ON, ROCK OFF – Duet

ARTICULATION: TENUTO AND STACCATO

Tenuto
Play with full value.

Staccato
Play light and separated.

5.25 LONG AND SHORT OF IT

TRACK **3** 25

HISTORY

MUSIC

Austrian composer **Franz Joseph Haydn** (1732 – 1809) is often referred to as the father of the symphony (He wrote 108 of them!). *Symphony No. 94* is often called the *Surprise Symphony*. Haydn surprised listeners with an unexpected loud chord that came after some very quiet music.

ART

Americans saw paintings by countryman John Trumbull (his historical painting *Declaration of Independence* is on the back of the $2 bill). In England, young artist Joseph Turner was setting the tone for Impressionism.

WORLD

The United States Bill of Rights was ratified, the world's first Sunday newspaper (*The Observer*) was published in England, and Benjamin Franklin invented bifocals!

5.26 SURPRISE SYMPHONY

Franz J. Haydn TRACK **3** 26

Andante

HISTORY

MUSIC

Paul Abraham Dukas (1865 – 1935) was a French composer who wrote in the Romantic style. His most famous work, *The Sorcerer's Apprentice,* is based on a poem by Johann Wolfgang von Goethe. The poem describes an apprentice who loses control of an enchanted broomstick.

ART

Edvard Munch, from Norway, painted in the Expressionist style which uses symbolism to portray many different themes. One of his best-known works is *The Scream* (1893).

WORLD

The 19th Amendment gave women the right to vote, author Madeleine L'Engle was born, and the first underground metro railway opened in Boston.

5.27 THE SORCERER'S APPRENTICE

Misterioso

Paul A. Dukas TRACK **3** 27

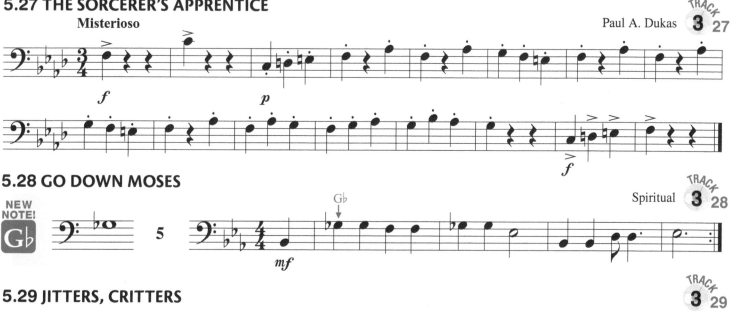

5.28 GO DOWN MOSES

Spiritual TRACK **3** 28

5.29 JITTERS, CRITTERS

TRACK **3** 29

Misterioso

BB208TBN

OPUS 5 ENCORE!

INTERPRETATION STATION

TRACK 3 30

Listen to CD 3 Track 30. For each example, decide if the articulation is *Legato* or *Staccato*.
Circle the letter that corresponds with your answer.

1. L   S   2. L   S   3. L   S   4. L   S

SIMON "SEZ"

TRACK 3 31

Listen to CD 3 Track 31. You will hear a well-known song. Listen first, sing it, then find the pitches on your instrument. You can then play along with the accompaniment track that follows. Can you match the notes and style of the initial recording?

COMPOSER'S CORNER

Writing a theme is just one part of a composer's process. Composers also use dynamics to make their music more expressive.
Add your own dynamics and then play the piece expressively. Choose from the following:

PENCIL POWER – MATCH THE STYLE TERMS

Match the style term with the correct definition by writing in the appropriate letter.

____ Legato

____ Maestoso

____ Dolce

____ Marziale

____ Cantabile

____ Calypso

A.   In a singing style

B.   In a march style

C.   Smooth and flowing

D.   Sweetly

E.   Blend of African and Caribbean music

F.   Majestically

CURTAIN UP!

5.30 LOCH LOMOND

Scottish Folk Song TRACK 3 32

5.31 LA MORISQUE (RENAISSANCE DANCE)

Tielman Susato
arr. Brian Balmages

TRACK 3 / 33

5.32 COSSACK'S MARCHING SONG

Russian Folk Song
arr. Robert Sheldon

TRACK 3 / 34

BB208TBN

✳ OPUS 6

THEORY

ENHARMONICS

Two notes that have the same pitch but different names are called **enharmonics**. An example would be G♭ and F♯.
They have different names but share the same slide position and sound the same when played!

6.1 ENHARMONIC ZONE

6.2 THE SPHINX

6.3 THE SPY

6.4 FINAL FRONTIER

6.5 MARCH SLAV
Pyotr I. Tchaikovsky

THEORY

DYNAMICS

pp (*pianissimo*) – play very soft

ff (*fortissimo*) – play very loud

6.6 ARIRANG
Korean Folk Song

HISTORY	MUSIC		ART	WORLD
	Italian born **Giuseppe Verdi** (1813 – 1901) is best known for his operas, especially *Il Trovatore* (The Troubadour), first performed in 1853. The *Anvil Chorus*, from Act 2 of *Il Trovatore*, features Spanish gypsies who sing and strike anvils as they work in the early morning.		Art in the style of Luminism began in the 1850s and was characterized by the use of light effects best seen in sea and landscapes. This American style is found in works by Frederic Church (*Twilight in the Wilderness*) and Martin Heade (*Sunlight and Shadow: The Newbury Marshes*).	In 1853, when *Il Trovatore* premiered, the Ottoman Empire declared war on Russia, the Gadsden Purchase (currently southern Arizona and New Mexico) was made, and potato chips made their first tasty appearance.

6.7 ANVIL CHORUS

Pesante *(heavily)*

Giuseppe Verdi — TRACK **3** 41

THEORY

MORE DYNAMICS

cresc.   Sometimes this abbreviation is used in place of a crescendo sign.
It means the same thing as the sign; gradually play louder.

decresc.   Sometimes this abbreviation is used in place of a decrescendo sign.
It means the same thing as the sign; gradually play softer.

6.8 YANKEE DOODLE CAME AND WENT

Moderato

American Folk Melody — TRACK **3** 42

THEORY

MAJOR SCALE, ARPEGGIO, AND CHORD

A **major scale** has eight notes going up or down in consecutive order, all in the key signature of the scale name.
In your key of B♭ Major, all eight notes are in the key signature of B♭ Major, which has 2 flats.
The top and bottom notes are both B♭. The distance between these notes is called an **octave**.

An **arpeggio** is the first, third, and fifth notes of a scale played in *succession*. It may also include the 8th scale note.

A **major chord** is the first, third, and fifth notes of a major scale played *simultaneously*.
Like the arpeggio, it may also include the 8th scale note.

6.9 CONCERT B♭ MAJOR SCALE

TRACK **3** 43

6.10 CONCERT B♭ MAJOR ARPEGGIO AND CHORD

TRACK **3** 44

6.11 KUM BAH YAH *Circle the arpeggios.* African Folk Song TRACK 3 45

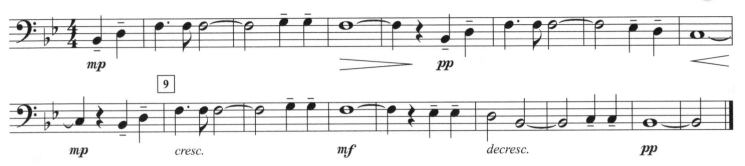

mp — *pp* — *mp* cresc. *mf* decresc. *pp*

INTERVALS

 THEORY

An **interval** is the distance between two pitches. You can figure out the interval by counting each line and space between the notes. Starting with "1" on the bottom note, count upward until you reach the top note. The number of the top note identifies the interval.

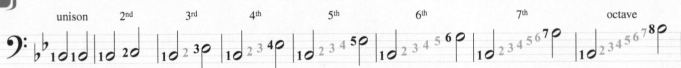

unison 2nd 3rd 4th 5th 6th 7th octave

6.12 RANGE ROVER 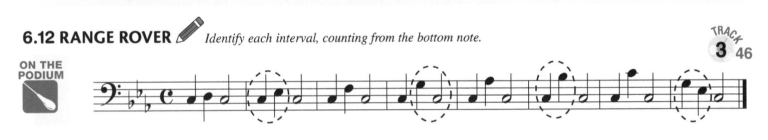 *Identify each interval, counting from the bottom note.* TRACK 3 46

ON THE PODIUM

6.13 HATIKVAH Israeli National Anthem TRACK 3 47

Andante

mp

mf

rit.

6.14 HEY! TRACK 3 48

ON THE PODIUM

Allegro

f

Hey!

MORE ABOUT SYNCOPATION

You already know the quarter-half-quarter syncopation. The most common syncopated rhythm is eighth-quarter-eighth. Here the syncopation occurs on the accented upbeat quarter note.

BB208TBN

6.21 DIES IRAE

Pesante

att. Thomas of Celano

6.22 LEAGUE OF SUPERHEROES

Allegro

CHROMATIC SCALE

A **half step** is the smallest interval between two pitches. Two consecutive half steps make a **whole step**.
The **chromatic scale** has thirteen notes going up and down in consecutive half steps.

6.23 CHROMATIC SCALE

no key signature!

HISTORY

MUSIC

Georges Bizet (1838 – 1875) was a child prodigy from Paris who composed his first symphony in 1855 when he was just 16! In his short 36-year life, he wrote many different types of music but is best known for his operas. His most famous opera is *Carmen*.

ART

The Impressionistic style was all the rage in the art world. Edgar Degas had painted *In Concert Cafe, The Song of the Dog*. American realist painter Thomas Eakins completed the *Gross Clinic*, a very real rendition of a surgeon overseeing an operation to remove part of a diseased thighbone.

WORLD

Events in 1875 included the first organized indoor ice hockey game in Montreal, the running of the first Kentucky Derby, and the patent of the electric dental drill.

6.24 HABAÑERA (FROM CARMEN) – Duet *Where is the ostinato?*

Georges Bizet

Moderato

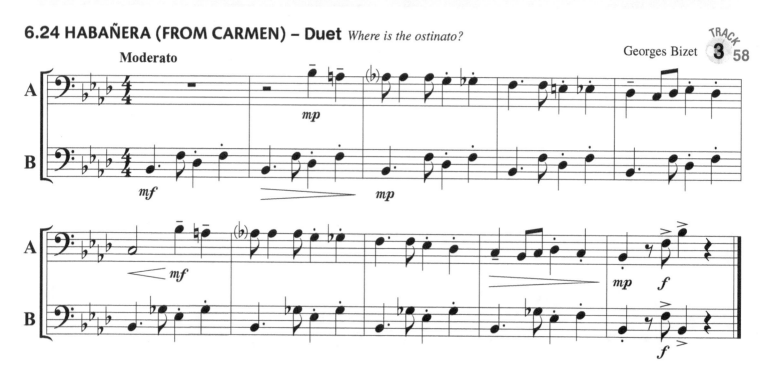

OPUS 6 ENCORE!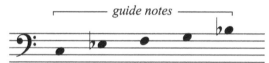

INTERPRETATION STATION

Listen to CD 3 Track 59. For each musical example, decide if the melody is based on a **Scale** or an **Arpeggio**.
Circle the letter that corresponds with your answer.

1. S A   2. S A   3. S A   4. S A

SIMON "SEZ"

Listen to CD 3 Track 60. You will hear a well-known piece. Listen first, sing it, then find the pitches on your instrument.
You can then play along with the accompaniment track that follows. Can you match the notes and style of the initial recording?

COMPOSER'S CORNER

Performers sometimes compose music on the spot while they are playing! This is called **improvisation.** There is an ostinato below.
Have a partner play it (or use CD 3 Track 61 as a background track) while you improvise. Use the guide notes to help you out. Have fun!
Note: The CD recording repeats 4 times.

"WHATEVER!"

PENCIL POWER

On the staff below, notate the enharmonic for each note. See if you can figure out the bonus notes!

CURTAIN UP!

6.25 O CANADA

Canadian National Anthem
Calixa Lavallée, Sir Adolphe-Basile Routhier, and Justice R.S. Weir

CURTAIN UP! FULL BAND

6.26 CHORALE IN Bb MAJOR
(ALLE MENSCHEN MÜSSEN STERBEN)

J. S. Bach

TRACK 3 63

6.27 RABBLE ROUSER

Robert Sheldon

TRACK 3 64

6.28 PROCESSION OF THE CHAMPIONS

Brian Balmages

TRACK **3** 65

BB208TBN

6.29 ROYAL MARCH OF THE LION
Instrumental Solo

Camille Saint-Saëns
arr. Brian Balmages

TRACK 3 66

Piano Accompaniment
Note: Sections are repeated in the accompaniment for spacing reasons and do not always follow the solo part.

TRACK 3 67

(Piano accompaniment only)

SCALES AND TECHNIQUE

CONCERT B♭ MAJOR

SCALE

SCALE IN THIRDS

CONCERT E♭ MAJOR

SCALE

SCALE IN THIRDS

CONCERT A♭ MAJOR

SCALE

SCALE IN THIRDS

CONCERT F MAJOR

SCALE

SCALE IN THIRDS

CHROMATIC SCALE

RHYTHM REVIEW – OPUS 1-6

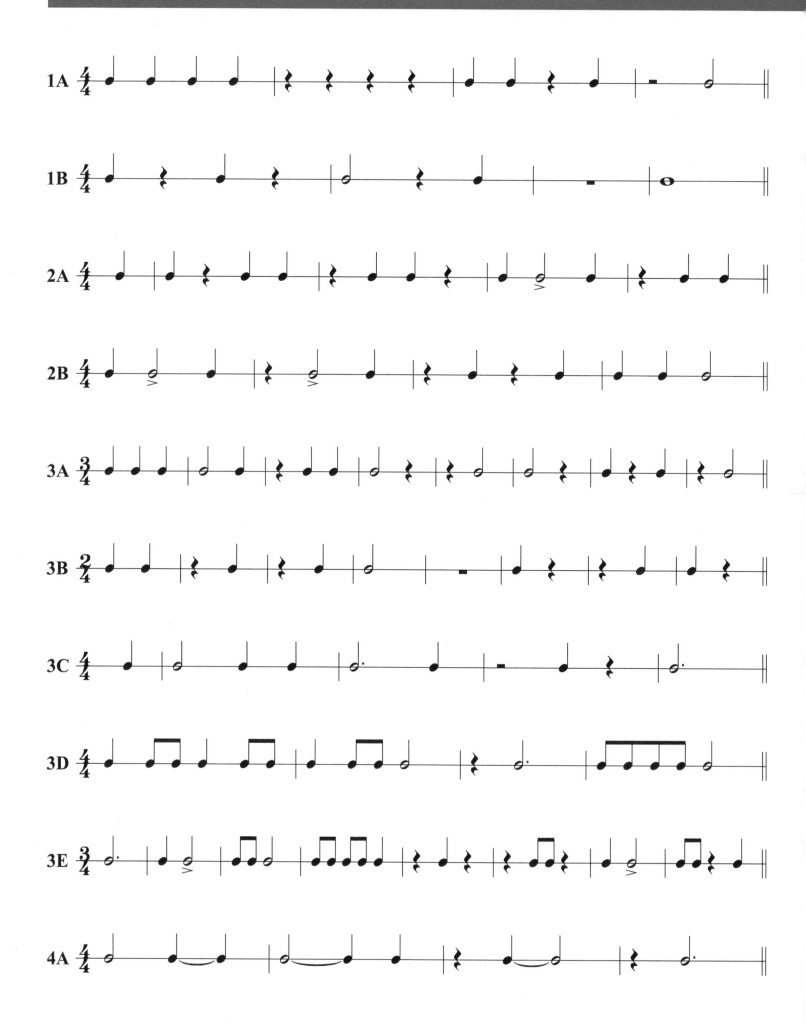

TROMBONE SLIDE POSITIONS

Numbers indicate slide positions.

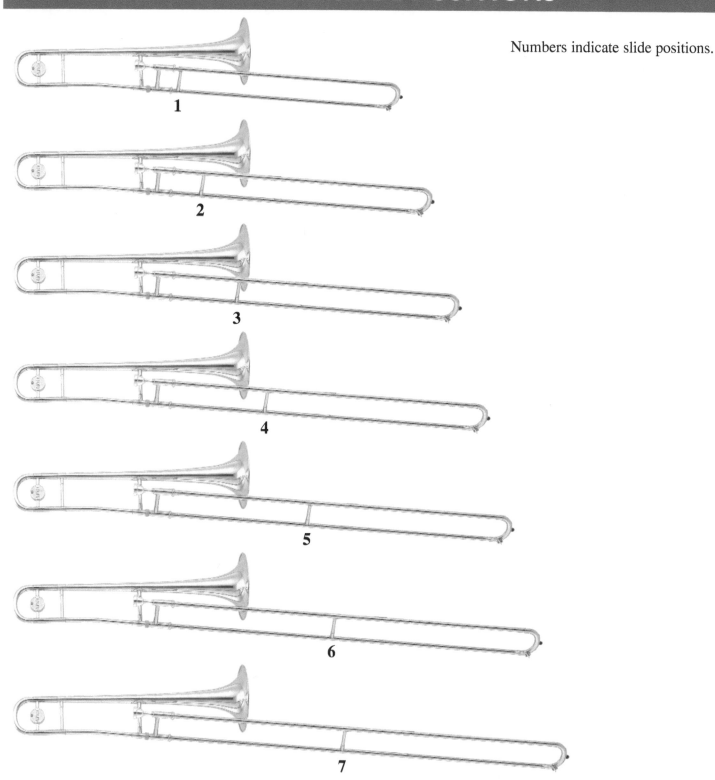

1

2

3

4

5

6

7

PRACTICING TIPS

Some exercises will be very easy for you to master while others will require more diligent practice. Be prepared to spend more time on the music that is difficult for you. Above all, be consistent in your approach and always end with something fun! The enclosed CDs are a great tool to help you practice, but it is important that you also practice alone.

- Find a **quiet place** where you can practice without distraction.
- Practice at the **same time each day** so it becomes part of your daily schedule.
- Use a **straight back chair** and a **music stand** to promote good posture.
- Begin with a **regular warm-up routine**.
- Practice your **lesson assignments** and **band music**, spending additional time on challenging sections.
- Wrap up your practice by playing **something fun**!

TROMBONE SLIDE POSITION CHART

Numbers indicate slide positions.

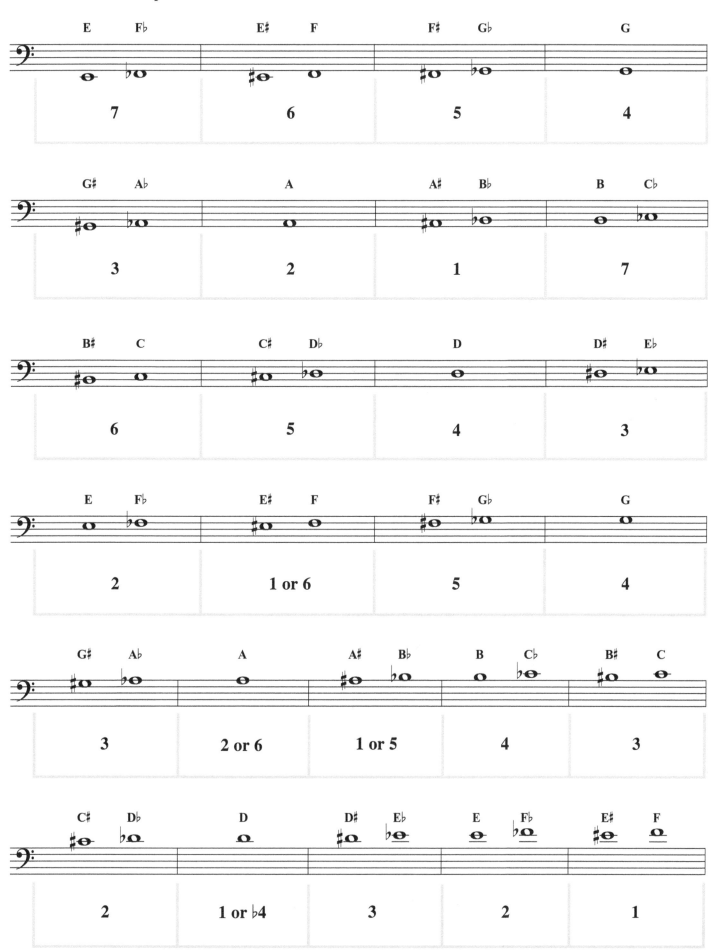

INDEX